THE ADAPTIVE REAL ESTATE AGENT

From Beginner To Expert In A Changing World

KENNETH LEONARDO

Copyright © 2024 Kenneth Leonardo

All rights reserved.

You cannot copy, replicate, or share the content of this book without getting written permission from the author or publisher.

Under no circumstances will any blame or legal responsibility be held against the publisher, or author, for any damages, reparation, or monetary loss due to the information contained within this book, either directly or indirectly.

Legal Notice:

This book is protected by copyright. It is for personal use only. You cannot change, share, sell, quote, or summarize any part of this book without permission from the author or publisher.

Disclaimer Notice:

The information in this document is for educational and entertainment purposes only. We have tried our best to provide accurate and reliable information. There are no guarantees of any kind. Readers understand that the author is not providing legal, financial, medical, or professional advice. The content in this book comes from various sources. Please talk to a licensed professional before trying any techniques mentioned in this book.

By reading this document, you agree that the author is not responsible for any losses, direct or indirect, that happen because of the information in this document, including mistakes, missing information, or inaccuracies.

DEDICATION

To my beloved wife, whose unwavering support and love have been my guiding light through every challenge.

CONTENTS

DEDICATION iii
AUTHOR'S NOTE vii
CHAPTER 1 1
    UNDERSTANDING THE REAL ESTATE LANDSCAPE AND SETTING REALISTIC GOALS 1
        IDENTIFYING PERSONAL STRENGTHS AND EMBRACING A LEARNER'S MINDSET 5
CHAPTER 2 11
    SELF-STARTER STRATEGIES 11
        ESTABLISHING EFFECTIVE ROUTINES AND TIME MANAGEMENT 13
        BUILDING RESILIENCE IN REAL ESTATE 17
CHAPTER 3 21
    NETWORKING AND COMMUNICATION MASTERY 21
        BUILDING A NETWORK AND EFFECTIVE COMMUNICATION 23
        LEVERAGING SOCIAL MEDIA FOR NETWORKING 26
CHAPTER 4 31
    THE POWER OF MENTORSHIP 31
        IDENTIFYING AND BUILDING RELATIONSHIPS WITH MENTORS 33
        MAXIMIZING LEARNING FROM MENTOR EXPERIENCES 37
CHAPTER 5 41
    BUILDING YOUR PERSONAL BRAND 41
        DEFINING YOUR UNIQUE VALUE PROPOSITION 43
        UTILIZING DIGITAL PLATFORMS FOR BRANDING 45
CHAPTER 6 50
    NURTURING CLIENT AND COLLEAGUE RELATIONSHIPS 50
        ACTIVE LISTENING, EMPATHY, AND MANAGING EXPECTATIONS 52
        BUILDING TRUST WITH COLLEAGUES AND TURNING CLIENTS INTO REPEAT BUSINESS 56

CHAPTER 7 60
   ACHIEVING WORK-LIFE BALANCE 60
      ESTABLISHING BOUNDARIES AND WELLNESS PRIORITIZATION 62
      INTEGRATING HEALTH AND PERSONAL INTERESTS 65
CHAPTER 8 69
   SUSTAINING SUCCESS 69
      CONTEMPLATING PERSONAL AND PROFESSIONAL
      DEVELOPMENT AND NURTURING SPIRITUAL PRACTICE 71
      STAYING ADAPTABLE IN A CHANGING INDUSTRY 74
   REFERENCES 79
ABOUT THE AUTHOR 87

AUTHOR'S NOTE

The inspiration for this book springs from my journey in real estate, which began in 2021 and continues to this day. My name is Kenneth Leonardo, and prior to embarking on a real estate career, I spent years at sea as a seafarer.

My extensive experience in hospitality, working alongside individuals from 44 different nationalities aboard a cruise ship, allowed me to explore numerous countries at a young age. This rich multicultural background has shaped my abilities in communication, networking, and the delicate art of listening.

I have channeled these skills into my pursuit of real estate, ultimately discovering that my true passion lies in serving others through my expertise and knowledge of real estate and life.

I also shared some of my technique here from a zero-knowledge real estate agent to becoming one of the top performing in a real estate developer; I hope this helps other real estate agent aspirants or existing agents who want to acquire some of the skills that I will share in this book.

CHAPTER 1

UNDERSTANDING THE REAL ESTATE LANDSCAPE AND SETTING REALISTIC GOALS

Entering the world of real estate can feel overwhelming, especially for beginners. However, by learning the fundamental aspects of this dynamic field and developing your goal-setting abilities, you can start a rewarding career. At its core, real estate focuses on creating matches between people and properties that fulfill their needs and desires. To do this effectively, it is essential to grasp the key features of the market. A detailed market analysis is crucial for anyone looking to succeed in real estate, whether in residential or commercial segments. The residential real estate market focuses on the buying and selling of homes, heavily influenced by factors such as location, neighborhood dynamics, and buyer demand. In contrast, the commercial sector encompasses office buildings, retail outlets, and industrial spaces, each presenting unique considerations. Keeping abreast of evolving trends in these markets enables agents and investors to make strategic decisions that align with current market realities and client expectations. For example, increasing urbanization may elevate the demand for condominiums, while shifts toward remote work could reshape the need for office environments. Acknowledging these changes empowers professionals to refine their approaches effectively.

A vital aspect of establishing a thriving real estate career is mastering industry terminology. The specialized language of real estate can be daunting, but grasping these terms enhances confidence and improves communication with clients and peers. Words like "equity," "amortization," and "staggered" may appear complicated at first glance, but with a little effort, their meanings become clear.

Understanding the vocabulary of real estate minimizes

confusion and fosters professionalism, leading to effective interactions and negotiations.

Knowing the market and terms is important, but understanding the rules is also essential. The real estate industry has many regulations to protect both agents and clients. Agents must know the licensing process, what information they must disclose, and fair housing laws. Understanding these rules helps avoid legal issues and builds trust with clients. Agents who are well-versed in these areas can establish strong, lasting relationships with their clients.

Establishing clear objectives is crucial for achieving success, going beyond just analyzing the market or understanding legal requirements. This is where the SMART framework becomes essential—crafting goals that are Specific, Measurable, Achievable, Relevant, and Time-bound. SMART goals serve as a precise guide, directing efforts and enabling the tracking of progress. For example, an emerging real estate agent might aim to finalize 8 sales in a year by focusing on particular neighborhoods with high turnover rates. This clarity makes the goal attainable and drives consistent action.

To effectively expand your professional network, implement a SMART approach by setting a clear goal for the number of new connections you aim to make or by deciding to join relevant industry groups within a specific timeline. This allows you to measure your progress precisely. You might also plan to attend a certain number of industry events each quarter. Additionally, utilize your social media channels to inform family, friends, and current contacts about your entry into real estate. By aligning these efforts with your primary career objectives—like increasing referrals or targeting a niche market—you can keep your focus sharp and your progress steady.

SMART goals provide a framework for long-term objectives, but it's also important to focus on short-term wins. Short-term goals serve as stepping stones, offering immediate motivation and reinforcing commitment. These can include mastering a specific contract form or reaching a monthly sales milestone. Celebrating these smaller achievements keeps enthusiasm high and builds momentum toward bigger goals. Rewarding yourself, like buying new clothes or shoes, can also boost your motivation by increasing your confidence and driving more sales.

Establishing SMART goals involves self-reflection and the ability to adapt. As market dynamics and personal situations change, it is essential for agents to regularly review and refine their objectives to ensure they align with feasible expectations. Being flexible is vital; for instance, with new uncertainties on the horizon, how can you attract more clients if you're not familiar with social media platforms. Responding swiftly to these fluctuations illustrates proactive decision-making and resilience. Like water, adaptability to your surroundings and making quick, informed decisions enhance your efficiency.

Ultimately, developing a mindset geared toward growth and adaptation is at the heart of beginning your journey in real estate. Embracing continuous learning through market research, networking opportunities, and skill enhancement courses expands your capabilities and positions you as a knowledgeable resource in your field. It also opens doors to innovative strategies, keeping you ahead of the curve amidst an ever-changing landscape.

IDENTIFYING PERSONAL STRENGTHS AND EMBRACING A LEARNER'S MINDSET

Self-assessment is the cornerstone of personal and professional growth, particularly for those embarking on new journeys, such as a career in real estate. By understanding areas of expertise and identifying growth opportunities, individuals can build confidence that propels informed decision-making for their development. Utilizing self-assessment tools allows individuals to explore latent skills and to recognize potential areas for improvement. These tools are vital in helping professionals navigate the vast realm of real estate by shedding light on personal strengths and weaknesses.

When starting out in real estate, engaging with various self-assessment tools can provide invaluable insights into where one naturally excels and where more effort may be necessary. Instruments like Myers-Briggs Type Indicator or StrengthsFinder serve as excellent guides to uncover personality traits and natural talents that align well with industry needs. This knowledge empowers aspiring real estate professionals to harness their strengths strategically while addressing areas that require enhancement. It also builds a foundation for confidence as they step into roles that match their skill sets effectively.

Creating a personalized development plan is an essential next step in this journey. Tailoring a development plan helps connect personal skill enhancement to career advancement, offering concrete steps tailored to individual needs. This involves setting clear objectives that align with career ambitions and evolving industry demands.

A well-structured plan focuses efforts on gaining the essential skills and experience required for thriving in real estate. This development plan acts as a roadmap, guiding individuals through their professional journeys with precision.

For instance, if someone identifies negotiation as a weak area through self-assessment, their plan might include enrolling in negotiation workshops or shadowing seasoned agents during client meetings. Such targeted actions ensure continuous improvement while keeping career goals in sight. Aligning personal development with career aspirations not only fuels motivation but also ensures long-term success as market dynamics evolve.

Feedback plays a crucial role in personal growth and should be sought regularly throughout one's career. Constructive criticism offers fresh perspectives and fosters relationships within the industry. It supports a culture of continuous improvement, encouraging individuals to refine their skills based on input from mentors, peers, and clients. Engaging in open dialogues about performance and potential growth areas nurtures collaboration and builds stronger networks within the real estate community.

Moreover, feedback should not be seen solely as a critique

but as a valuable opportunity to gain insights into how others perceive your abilities. Regular interactions with experienced colleagues and participation in real estate forums can provide candid opinions that highlight both strengths and areas needing attention. By embracing feedback, individuals can make informed adjustments to their approach, enhancing their effectiveness and reputation in the field.

Cultivating curiosity is another essential aspect of encouraging continuous learning and adaptation. In the dynamic world of real estate, staying engaged in conversations and accessing diverse resources is vital. Curiosity drives proactive learning, ensuring that professionals remain knowledgeable about emerging trends, market shifts, and innovative practices. It encourages individuals to view mistakes as learning opportunities, fostering resilience and adaptability.

Being curious means never settling for a surface-level understanding. Instead, it involves diving deep into industry literature, attending seminars, and participating in discussions with peers and experts alike. By continuously seeking knowledge, real estate professionals keep themselves ahead of the curve, ready to tackle any challenges that arise. This proactive approach to learning positions them as thought leaders who confidently lead clients through complex transactions.

To support these developmental pathways, integrating learning resources into everyday routines is critical. Professionals must leverage a mix of formal training programs, mentorship initiatives, and self-directed studies to stay relevant. Accessing online courses, webinars, and books related to real estate can supplement on-the-job experiences, providing a comprehensive learning ecosystem. Learning doesn't stop at initial education; it's a lifelong pursuit that enriches careers and enhances adaptability to change.

Overcoming the fear of failure is equally important on this growth journey. Mistakes and failures should be viewed as integral components of learning rather than setbacks. Embracing a mindset that sees value in every misstep encourages experimentation and innovation. The real estate industry thrives on creative solutions and novel approaches, which often arise from lessons learned during failures. By normalizing the idea that failure is a part of the process, individuals can push boundaries without the paralyzing fear of making mistakes.

Failure experiences teach resilience and inspire unique

problem-solving strategies, essential traits for any successful real estate professional. Each challenge encountered and overcome adds to a growing toolbox of skills and insights. Encouraging a culture where trial and error are celebrated fosters an environment ripe for personal and collective growth.

CHAPTER 2

SELF-STARTER STRATEGIES

Cultivating the habits and mindset necessary to thrive as a self-starting real estate agent is an essential journey for those entering or transitioning within this dynamic industry. At its core, this chapter focuses on uncovering the strategies that empower individuals to take the initiative in their professional endeavors.

Becoming self-reliant involves more than just ambition; it's about equipping oneself with the tools and attitudes required to turn aspirations into tangible accomplishments.

By delving into these strategies, readers will discover how to harness innate potential and drive themselves forward with confidence and clarity. This exploration is crucial for new entrants eager to navigate the complexities of real estate and for professionals in transition looking to effectively adapt their existing skills to a fresh landscape.

In this chapter, readers will be guided through various self-starter strategies tailored to fortify an individual's proactive capabilities in real estate. The discussions here will illuminate the importance of establishing effective routines and mastering time management, essential elements for maintaining focus amidst myriad responsibilities. Readers will learn the significance of reflection and goal-setting as foundational practices to keep motivation high and ensure continuous progress.

Additionally, practical insights into structuring days for maximum efficiency and developing resilience against common industry challenges will be covered. These strategic approaches aim to provide a comprehensive framework for cultivating self- sufficiency and thriving as a self-starting agent in the real estate field. Through these discussions, aspiring agents can gain valuable knowledge to bolster their confidence and prepare them to make meaningful strides in their careers.

ESTABLISHING EFFECTIVE ROUTINES AND TIME MANAGEMENT

Harnessing a well-structured day can be transformative for those entering or transitioning into real estate. Implementing a routine effectively manages your time, focusing on essential tasks while simultaneously minimizing stress. The essence of a structured day lies in its ability to streamline your energy towards activities that foster growth and productivity in this dynamic field.

A structured routine is vital in enhancing how time is utilized, significantly impacting an agent's efficiency. Consider the demands of real estate: managing client interactions, overseeing property listings, negotiating deals, and continually expanding networks. Without a clear structure, it's easy to feel overwhelmed, unable to prioritize crucial tasks over less important distractions.

By organizing your day, you allocate dedicated time slots to high-priority activities, reducing decision fatigue and diminishing stress associated with disorganized work patterns.

This systematic approach ensures you're focused when it matters most, like during negotiations or client meetings, avoiding last-minute rushes and enhancing your professional image. Incorporating goal-setting into daily routines acts as a motivational beacon, guiding agents toward achieving specific objectives.

Setting distinct goals each day gives clarity and directs your efforts where they're needed most. For instance, if the aim is to close three property deals within a month, breaking down the target into daily actionable steps—perhaps contacting ten potential clients daily—makes the ambition seem less daunting and more achievable. Beyond just motivation, having these goals allows agents to track progress, offering a sense of accomplishment as milestones are reached, reinforcing positive habits over time.

Creating specific time blocks for different activities within your schedule enhances overall efficiency. Time blocking involves setting aside particular periods for dedicated tasks, such as prospecting, client meetings, follow-ups, and administrative duties.

This method helps avoid multitasking pitfalls, allowing full concentration on one task at a time. Moreover, by designating time for personal activities, it promotes work-life balance, which is crucial for maintaining long-term satisfaction and preventing burnout.

A simple yet practical guideline here is to evaluate your natural energy levels throughout the day and align demanding tasks with peak performance times, ensuring you're working smarter, not harder (Arlinghaus & Johnston, 2018).

Reflection time, although often overlooked, is a powerful component for continuous improvement in this field. Establishing regular intervals for reflection enables agents to pause and assess their strategies and outcomes. By dedicating moments for introspection, agents can identify what's working well and what requires modification, thus fostering mindful growth and adaptability. This practice aids in refining techniques, learning from experiences, and aligning future actions with overarching career goals. Integrating reflection doesn't necessitate lengthy sessions; even brief end- of-day reviews can yield significant insights into personal and professional development.

Let's consider how these principles converge in a typical week's schedule for a budding real estate professional. Start each day with a short goal- setting session. Clearly defining what needs to be accomplished provides a roadmap for the day's activities and keeps motivation levels high. As you move through your day, adhere to predefined time blocks. For example, dedicate the morning hours—when mental acuity is typically highest—to client calls or challenging negotiations. Allocate afternoons for property showings or networking events, utilizing the peak social energy suited for interpersonal engagements.

Throughout your routine, remain flexible enough to adapt when necessary. Real estate is an industry known for its unpredictability; thus, being too rigid can lead to missed opportunities or unnecessary stress. Incorporate buffer times between tasks to accommodate unforeseen changes without derailing your entire day. Regularly review your progress against set goals, using reflection periods strategically placed at the end of each week. This practice not only sheds light on accomplishments but also highlights areas ripe for improvement.

Finally, remember that developing a new routine is a gradual process, one that requires patience and persistence. It takes time for any habit to take root deeply enough to become second nature. According to experts, complex habits may take longer to form than simpler ones, so allow yourself grace as you navigate this journey towards a more structured day (Arlinghaus & Johnston, 2018).

BUILDING RESILIENCE IN REAL ESTATE

Navigating the challenges and developing resilience as a self-starting real estate agent can be likened to sailing through a constantly changing sea. It requires adaptive strategies and foresight, geared towards turning potential hurdles into stepping stones for growth. Recognizing common obstacles in the industry forms the bedrock of proactive anticipation, allowing agents to develop solutions even before issues arise, creating an environment where shared experiences pave the way for collective learning.

Real estate often presents unique challenges, from market fluctuations to managing client expectations. By identifying these common obstacles early, new agents can plot strategic courses to mitigate their impact. Understanding that these barriers are not isolated incidents but shared stories within the industry allows for a sense of camaraderie among professionals. It's like knowing the tides; once familiar, you can navigate them more effectively. Recognition of these patterns ensures that facing difficulties becomes less daunting and more about seeking innovative solutions.

A crucial part of thriving amidst obstacles is cultivating resilience. Resilience isn't just about bouncing back; it's a dynamic process of adapting well in the face of adversity. For real estate agents, this means maintaining motivation and seeing each setback as an avenue for further improvement. Strategies for building resilience are manifold but essential in ensuring sustained success. This includes embedding a mindset where challenges are no longer seen as burdens but rather as opportunities for personal and professional growth. When adversity hits, resilient agents don't merely survive—they thrive by finding new ways to approach problems.

To strengthen resilience, one must embrace a paradigm shift—seeing failures not as defeats but as valuable lessons. Each misstep offers insights that contribute to future achievements. Imagine setbacks as rough sketches that eventually shape the masterpiece of your career. Learning from failure is crucial, and it's a practice that emphasizes self-reflection and ongoing development. Acceptance of past mistakes without harsh self-judgment fosters a nurturing environment for creativity and innovation, leading to newfound pathways in one's professional journey.

Building a robust support network is another significant strategy for resilience that should not be overlooked. Peers and mentors play a pivotal role in encouraging collaboration, offering fresh perspectives, and infusing agents with renewed vigor when faced with challenges. In real estate, a well-connected agent is like a tree with deep roots— firmly grounded yet flexible enough to withstand strong winds. Networking facilitates sharing ideas and resources, helping agents overcome isolation and gain insights from others' experiences. It's about creating a safety net, much like a supportive community, to bolster confidence during unforeseen trials.

Moreover, mentors offer guidance drawn from years of experience, providing strategies that have stood the test of time. Their role is akin to a lighthouse, guiding newcomers through turbulent waters. Regular interactions with mentors and peers enhance problem-solving capabilities, reduce stress, and provide emotional support, making the navigation of the real estate landscape less overwhelming.

While conquering challenges is fundamental, cultivating resilience remains integral. Implementing guidelines that foster this quality involves not just individual actions but also leveraging collective strength. As per the research, practical strategies such as developing self- awareness and emotional intelligence are vital tools for enhancing resilience. These attributes enable agents to manage stress, maintain clarity during crises, and inspire those around them.

Setting realistic goals serves as a cornerstone for resilience. A clear objective provides purpose and direction, enabling agents to remain focused amid adversity. The concept of breaking down long-term aspirations into smaller, achievable steps enhances productivity and keeps enthusiasm alive. Each completed task is a testament to perseverance, reinforcing belief in one's ability to conquer obstacles. This incremental progress builds a sense of accomplishment, fueling determination to advance despite hurdles.

Additionally, promoting a healthy work-life balance is essential. Balancing personal and professional life nurtures well-being and sustains passion for the job, which translates into heightened performance and engagement. It prevents burnout, ensuring that agents are always at their best when tackling challenges head-on.

CHAPTER 3

NETWORKING AND COMMUNICATION MASTERY

Mastering networking and communication in real estate is essential for anyone looking to thrive in this dynamic industry.

Effective networking goes beyond just knowing people—it involves building meaningful relationships that can provide insights, opportunities, and collaborations valuable to your career. This chapter delves into the nuances of networking by exploring how to identify and connect with key individuals who can support your professional journey.

It emphasizes the importance of intentional relationship-building strategies, such as attending industry events with a purpose, engaging with peers meaningfully, and leveraging existing networks to expand your reach and establish credibility.

Additionally, the chapter highlights the vital role of communication in the realm of real estate. It guides you through the art of active listening and how it can transform ordinary interactions into personalized experiences, thereby fostering trust and understanding with clients. You'll also discover techniques for clear and concise messaging, ensuring that your ideas are easily understood when shared with clients or partners.

This section underscores the power of storytelling, presenting how sharing relatable narratives can make your interactions memorable and impactful. Finally, the chapter will address the importance of regular follow-ups in maintaining strong relationships, reinforcing the idea that effective communication is not just about speaking but also about nurturing connections for long-term success.

BUILDING A NETWORK AND EFFECTIVE COMMUNICATION

Mastering networking and communication skills is essential, particularly for those entering the intricate realm of real estate. Whether you are new to the field, shifting from a different profession, or looking to enhance your current connections, developing these skills is key to achieving success.

Effective networking goes beyond simply making contacts; it requires a thorough understanding of how to communicate with them. Additionally, mastering the art of listening is crucial, as it allows you to uncover clients' challenges, financial commitments, interests, and aspirations, helping you find common ground and build trust.

To begin with, identifying your target audience is crucial. Think about who you need to connect with—this could include potential clients, fellow real estate professionals, or industry influencers. Focus on making connections that align with your professional goals. Identifying the right people allows you to concentrate your efforts where they matter most. For instance, if you aim to specialize in commercial real estate, connecting with business owners and developers would be more beneficial than focusing solely on residential buyers.

Participating in industry events is an excellent strategy to build your network. These events provide opportunities to meet peers who can offer valuable insights and potentially collaborate with you on projects. When you attend such events, approach them with a mindset oriented towards learning and growth. Make it a point to engage in discussions, share your perspectives, and listen to others. This active participation doesn't just offer immediate knowledge but also positions you as someone invested in the industry's broader dialogue.

Beyond forming new connections, fostering existing relationships is equally important. Requesting introductions through mutual contacts and obtaining recommendations can significantly enhance trust among your network. Recommendations act as endorsements, which can open doors to new partnerships and clientele. Trust and credibility grow from these established networks, creating a foundation upon which you can build your reputation.

A significant part of effective communication within networking is mastering the art of active listening. Understanding your clients' needs is paramount for presenting solutions that truly add value. Listening actively involves engaging in conversations without distractions, asking questions to deepen your understanding, and reflecting back what you've heard to confirm accuracy. This approach not only demonstrates respect and attentiveness but also enables you to tailor your services to exactly what your client is looking for.

Active listening can transform a standard interaction into a deeply personalized experience for your clients. It signals that their concerns and ambitions are your priorities, leading to better business relationships and more successful outcomes. In real estate, where every deal hinges on a multitude of specifics, understanding and responding appropriately to needs can set you apart from the competition.

Moreover, developing clear and concise messaging is essential when communicating in professional settings. Real estate can be filled with jargon and complex information, so the ability to express ideas simply and understandably can greatly impact how your message is received. Practicing clarity in your communications not only helps in direct interactions but also improves your overall professional image. Clear messaging fosters better comprehension and decision-making among your clients and partners.

Employing storytelling techniques to communicate your messages can be highly effective. Individuals commonly recall narratives more vividly than isolated facts or statistics. Illustrating experiences from previous transactions or case studies where you've assisted clients in overcoming obstacles can make your presentation more relatable and impactful. Narratives invoke emotions and foster connections that data alone often fails to achieve, enabling your audience to visualize the advantages of collaborating with you. Always use imagery to express your ideas when sending messages; this will help them visualize the values you aim to convey.

Finally, the practice of following up regularly with your network is key to maintaining and strengthening those relationships. Regular follow- ups show that you value the relationship beyond initial interactions. A simple thank-you email after a meeting or a check-in call can reinforce your interest in a continued partnership. These gestures keep the lines of communication open and lay the groundwork for future collaborations

LEVERAGING SOCIAL MEDIA FOR NETWORKING

Utilizing social media as a strategic tool for expanding your network is an essential skill in the real estate industry. Social media platforms are not only abundant but also diverse, offering plenty of opportunities to connect with like-minded individuals and potential clients. By selecting suitable social media platforms that align with your target demographic and industry focus, you can effectively expand your network and make meaningful connections.

First off, it's important to choose the right platforms based on where your audience spends their time. For those interested in engaging with other professionals and showcasing expertise, LinkedIn is a prime platform. It offers tools to build professional credibility by sharing achievements, experiences, and industry insights. On the other hand, Instagram and Facebook are excellent for reaching broader audiences through visually appealing content and interactive engagements. Determining where to invest your efforts will depend on understanding your specific goals and your audience's preferences.

Make your own personal page using a social media platform and website so people will know you and share the journey of each investor, allowing them to relate to you and always remember you by having your own tagline.

Once you've established your presence on the right platforms, consistently sharing insightful content is key to establishing authority. This doesn't mean bombarding your audience with posts, but rather providing value through well-thought-out content. Whether it's a detailed analysis of market trends or tips for first-time homebuyers, your content should resonate with your audience's needs and interests. By becoming a go-to resource for reliable information, you naturally attract more connections and followers who view you as an industry leader.

Engagement is another pillar of successful networking on social media. Beyond just posting, it's crucial to actively participate by commenting on and sharing others' posts. Such interactions demonstrate goodwill and open doors for collaboration opportunities. This reciprocal approach to engagement fosters a community spirit and helps you stay top-of-mind within your network. When you contribute meaningfully to discussions, or support others by sharing their content, you lay the groundwork for mutually beneficial relationships that can enhance your career prospects.

Moreover, building an authentic online presence is vital for attracting potential clients. Transparency is key here; people are more likely to trust someone who appears genuine and forthcoming. Share behind-the-scenes tidbits about your journey in real estate, lessons learned, and personal anecdotes that convey your personality and values. This not only makes you relatable but also differentiates you from those who overly curate their online personas. Authenticity builds credibility, which is critical in an industry where trust and reputation are paramount.

Personalizing interactions can also significantly impact your networking success. Tailor your messages to reflect genuine interest in the individual's work, background, or recent achievements. Instead of sending generic connection requests, mention something specific that caught your eye—a post they shared or mutual connections, for instance. Personal touches like these show that you're interested in more than just expanding your contact list; you're invested in forming real connections.

Also, don't underestimate the power of following up after meetings or transactions. A simple thank-you message expressing appreciation for someone's time can leave a lasting impression. If appropriate, suggest ways you might collaborate or offer something of value in return, like introducing them to your own network or sharing relevant resources. This act of maintaining the relationship shows your commitment to nurturing long-term professional bonds, setting the stage for future opportunities.

While organizing client appreciation events might seem like a step outside of social media strategy, it complements your online efforts by reinforcing relationships in a tangible way. These events need not be extravagant; even informal gatherings provide avenues for deeper engagement and can humanize your brand. Social media can aid in planning such events by gauging interest through polls or creating private groups to coordinate details. Showcasing snippets from these events online further amplifies your authenticity and dedication to client satisfaction.

CHAPTER 4

THE POWER OF MENTORSHIP

Mentoring is a powerful tool in shaping a successful real estate career. The value of mentorship lies in the wealth of experience and insight that seasoned professionals can impart to those entering the field. By tapping into this reservoir of knowledge, individuals new to real estate stand to significantly accelerate their learning curve and development. Aligning oneself with mentors who have navigated the complexities of the industry leads to unique opportunities for growth and progress. This connection with experienced guides nurtures an environment where mentees can gain not only practical skills but also strategic insights essential for thriving in a competitive marketplace. Mentorship is much more than a transfer of expertise; it involves creating supportive, reciprocal relationships that foster both personal and professional development.

In this chapter, readers will explore strategies for identifying and building relationships with the right mentors. It delves into the process of finding mentors whose experience matches the mentee's aspirations while highlighting key traits that make effective mentors, such as empathy and the capacity to provide constructive feedback. Additionally, the text examines how to leverage professional networks to uncover mentoring opportunities, emphasizing the importance of evaluating alignment between personal values and those of potential mentors.

Readers will learn about making compelling approaches to mentors, ensuring a fit that optimizes the benefits of the relationship. The narrative further discusses how mentors support evolving skillsets by providing invaluable feedback and guidance, crafted with real-world scenarios and illustrative examples. By engaging with these ideas, aspiring real estate professionals will equip themselves with the tools to build meaningful mentor-mentee partnerships, setting the stage for long-term success in the industry.

IDENTIFYING AND BUILDING RELATIONSHIPS WITH MENTORS

In navigating a real estate career, finding and forming effective relationships with mentors can be pivotal. Identifying suitable mentors is the first crucial step. It's essential to seek individuals who possess notable experience in the real estate sector along with empathy and openness to offering constructive feedback. These characteristics help ensure that your mentor not only understands the intricacies of the industry but also appreciates your personal journey and provides valuable guidance.

Research supports the importance of these traits, highlighting that mentors who are genuine, understanding, and supportive foster strong emotional connections and trust. Look for mentors with a successful track record in real estate, as their practical knowledge and insights can provide you with tangible strategies to succeed in the field.

Another key aspect to consider when identifying mentors is evaluating their ability to offer constructive feedback. Feedback is integral to growth and development, allowing you to refine your skills and adapt to challenges in real estate. Effective mentors provide regular feedback, challenge your assumptions, and encourage you to expand your professional networks and gain new experiences. Understanding mentor characteristics helps to identify potential mentors and evaluate whether they align with your personal values and aspirations. Aligning your values and goals with those of your mentor is another vital component of building a compatible relationship.

Enter the realm of professional networks to discover potential mentors by attending industry events, engaging on social media, or participating in local groups related to real estate. Networking opportunities facilitate connections with seasoned professionals who can guide your career trajectory.

Events such as real estate conferences, workshops, or seminars are invaluable spaces to meet mentors actively seeking to impart their knowledge and experiences. Similarly, platforms like LinkedIn or industry-specific forums can serve as gateways to connect with experts willing to share their expertise and perspectives. Utilizing these avenues broadens your reach, enabling you to uncover potential mentors who resonate with your professional goals.

Establishing a sense of fit and compatibility with a mentor goes beyond evaluating their skills and experience. It involves aligning personal values and goals with those of the mentor, ensuring a harmonious mentoring relationship. For example, if you aspire to specialize in residential properties, it would be advantageous to seek a mentor whose expertise aligns with this area. A mentor who shares similar values and interests will likely comprehend your ambitions better, providing more tailored advice and support. This alignment fosters a productive mentoring relationship, where both parties benefit from shared insights and experiences.

Approaching potential mentors requires thoughtful preparation. Crafting a compelling introduction is fundamental to capturing their attention and demonstrating your eagerness to learn. It's important to articulate your intentions clearly, expressing why you've chosen them specifically as a mentor. Acknowledge their achievements in the real estate industry and how you believe their guidance could enhance your professional growth.

Additionally, find common ground by exploring mutual interests or connections, creating a relatable foundation for your relationship. Demonstrating enthusiasm and respect for their time underscores your commitment to learning, increasing the likelihood of establishing a meaningful mentorship.

Mentorship fundamentally thrives on a dynamic where both mentor and mentee contribute actively. As you seek a mentor, remember that the relationship should be mutually beneficial. While mentors provide guidance and direction, mentees bring fresh perspectives and energy into the exchange.

Showing gratitude for their insights and taking proactive steps based on their feedback reinforces the value they add to your career development. Additionally, maintaining consistent and reliable contact ensures a robust and ongoing relationship, essential for fostering trust and collaboration.

Understanding the phases of a mentoring relationship can also offer valuable insights into managing expectations and ensuring its effectiveness. From initiation, where the relationship begins to form, to cultivation, where both personal and professional capabilities expand, each phase represents opportunities for growth and adaptation.

Being aware of these stages allows you to navigate transitions smoothly, sustaining a productive and fulfilling mentorship over time.

Mentors play a multifaceted role in shaping your real estate career, acting as ethical role models while inspiring and encouraging you to realize your potential. By helping you understand the professional culture and dynamics of the industry, they equip you with the tools needed to navigate challenges effectively. Moreover, mentors often open doors to new experiences and skill development, further enhancing your readiness to excel in real estate.

MAXIMIZING LEARNING FROM MENTOR EXPERIENCES

Active learning from mentors' experiences and insights is a powerful approach for those striving to excel in the real estate industry. It involves a deep engagement with what mentors impart, allowing mentees to internalize wisdom and implement it effectively.

To begin with, active listening is a foundational technique that facilitates this process. It requires not just hearing words but fully absorbing and understanding the mentor's advice. Active listening is characterized by paying close attention, maintaining eye contact, and providing feedback like nodding or summarizing points, which indicates genuine interest and comprehension. For instance, when a mentor provides insight on navigating market trends, actively listen by asking clarifying questions such as "Could you elaborate on how I might apply this strategy in my context?"

Furthermore, taking proactive steps based on feedback underscores commitment and initiative. When a mentor offers constructive criticism, it's essential to translate this into action. If a mentor suggests enhancing negotiation skills, one could enroll in workshops or practice role-playing scenarios with peers. By demonstrating initiative in refining skills mentioned by your mentor, you not only improve your capabilities but also show your dedication to growing professionally.

Documenting and regularly reviewing lessons learned is another critical practice. This process solidifies understanding and fosters deeper discussions. By maintaining a journal or digital notes of key takeaways from mentoring sessions, you create a valuable resource for future reference. Regular reviews of these insights help reinforce learning and prepare you to contribute meaningfully in subsequent discussions. A documented reflection on your mentor's guidance about client relations, for example, can be revisited before engaging with new clients to ensure you apply the best practices gleaned during mentoring.

Another effective strategy is seeking diverse perspectives through multiple mentors. Engaging with various mentors provides a broader range of insights and opinions, enriching your learning experience. Each mentor may bring a unique viewpoint based on their background and expertise. By connecting with different mentors, you gain a more nuanced understanding of the industry. Encouraging peer mentoring, where fellow real estate professionals share experiences and advice, further diversifies the knowledge pool. In doing so, you expose yourself to a multitude of strategies and solutions, enabling a more robust approach to challenges you might face.

Connecting with a variety of mentors also reinforces the value of diverse opinions in shaping your career path. For instance, one mentor may specialize in commercial real estate, while another excels in residential properties. By drawing from both, you can develop a comprehensive strategy that leverages insights from each area, thereby crafting a well-rounded approach to your career in real estate. This exposure helps in building flexibility and adaptability, crucial traits for thriving in an ever-evolving industry landscape.

The application of active learning extends beyond individual growth; it contributes significantly to establishing a culture of mentorship within professional networks. By immersing oneself in a mentorship framework characterized by active listening, proactive implementation, documentation, and diverse interactions, you become not only a recipient of wisdom but also an advocate for mentorship. Sharing these techniques with peers and encouraging them to adopt similar approaches amplifies the benefits, creating a supportive environment where everyone has the opportunity to learn and grow.

It's important to understand that mentorship is not a passive reception of advice but a dynamic interaction involving effort and responsiveness. The relationship between mentor and mentee thrives on mutual respect and understanding. By showing appreciation for your mentor's time and effort through active participation, you foster a productive mentorship environment that benefits both parties.

CHAPTER 5

BUILDING YOUR PERSONAL BRAND

Building your personal brand is paramount to making a lasting impression in any industry, but it's especially crucial in the competitive world of real estate. As someone new to the field or transitioning from a different career, you may wonder how you can differentiate yourself and leave a memorable mark on potential clients. This task begins with introspection—understanding your unique experiences and skills that set you apart from others in the market. By recognizing these attributes, whether it's a particular expertise or a fresh perspective, you can start crafting a brand that communicates these strengths in a compelling manner. What makes this endeavor exciting is the opportunity it presents to explore within yourself the qualities and stories that make you truly unique, turning them into professional assets.

The process of building a distinctive personal brand involves several strategic steps that will be explored in depth throughout this chapter. We'll guide you through the journey of defining your Unique Value Proposition (UVP), which serves as the foundation of your brand by highlighting what makes you indispensable. You'll learn how to tailor your approach to meet the specific needs of diverse client bases, ensuring that your services resonate with each segment individually.

Furthermore, we delve into the art of creating impactful elevator pitches and the power of storytelling as part of your branding strategy. These elements, when combined, help to foster emotional connections with clients, establishing trust and rapport. Through practical strategies and real-world examples, this chapter aims to equip you with the knowledge and tools necessary to build a personal brand that not only stands out in the real estate industry but also promises long-term success and fulfillment.

DEFINING YOUR UNIQUE VALUE PROPOSITION

In the bustling realm of real estate, establishing a distinctive personal brand is key to standing out and resonating with clients. Articulating what sets you apart involves a deep dive into your unique skills and experiences. Begin by identifying these distinguishing features. Think about feedback from past transactions—have clients consistently praised your ability to negotiate stellar deals? Perhaps your knack for uncovering hidden gem properties has been highlighted. This self-assessment not only sharpens your awareness but also pinpoints the competencies that set you apart from competitors.

Understanding your strengths becomes a roadmap to crafting your identity in the market. For aspiring agents or those transitioning careers, leveraging previous experience or transferable skills can create a powerful narrative. Maybe you've honed your negotiation prowess in sales roles outside real estate, or your background in architecture provides a unique perspective on property potential. Highlighting these elements within your Unique Value Proposition (UVP) allows you to offer clients something unique. This distinct blend captures what others cannot replicate, making your services not just different, but indispensable.

The next step involves tailoring your approach to meet the specific needs of potential clients. Real estate is not a one-size-fits-all industry; understanding client aspirations and challenges is crucial. If you're meeting first-time homebuyers, empathize with their anxieties and address them with patience and informative guidance.

On the other hand, investors might seek detailed market analytics and sound financial advice. Tailor your conversations and presentations to show how your strengths directly address their particular concerns. This adaptability builds trust and fosters engagement, as clients will see you not just as an agent, but as a problem solver dedicated to fulfilling their individual needs.

Creating a compelling elevator pitch is essential in communicating your value succinctly. This pitch should encapsulate your UVP in a manner that grabs attention while providing clarity. Imagine this scenario: you're at a networking event, surrounded by potential clients and partners. How do you convey your essence in thirty seconds? Focus on a few high-impact sentences. Let's say your strength lies in data-driven insights; a pitch could be, "I use in-depth market analysis to ensure my clients get the best value for their investments, whether they're buying or selling.

Beyond pitches, fostering emotional connections through storytelling is an impactful branding strategy. Narrate your journey in the real estate world—share the passion that ignited your career, the challenges overcome, and the triumphs achieved. This narrative doesn't merely appeal to logic but evokes emotions, building rapport with clients. A story about how you helped a family find their dream home despite market challenges can resonate deeply, engendering trust and loyalty. It establishes you as more than just an agent; you become a trusted advisor and a part of their success story.

As you define and communicate your personal brand, remember that authenticity is paramount. Genuine representation of who you are reflects honesty and integrity. Clients are increasingly savvy and can discern when someone is putting on a façade. Be true to your values and let them shine through in every interaction. This authenticity not only enhances your credibility but ensures that your professional journey is fulfilling and sustainable.

UTILIZING DIGITAL PLATFORMS FOR BRANDING

In today's digitally driven world, building a personal brand as a real estate agent has never been more crucial. Digital platforms offer unprecedented opportunities to showcase your unique offerings and connect with potential clients on a level that traditional marketing methods simply can't match. Leveraging these platforms effectively can transform how you engage with your audience and establish your presence in the competitive real estate market.

A cornerstone of any digital branding strategy is developing a user-friendly website designed to be the central hub of information for your clients. Your website should highlight your services, showcase property listings, and include testimonials from satisfied clients to build trust and credibility.

A well-designed website serves as a 24/7 storefront, offering visitors comprehensive insights into your expertise and the superior experience they can expect when working with you. In this light, ensuring your site is mobile-responsive is critical; as noted by "The Ultimate Guide to Digital Marketing in Real Estate," nearly 77% of consumers use their mobile devices to search for properties online. Thus, your website needs to be visually appealing and function seamlessly across all devices to capture and retain the attention of potential buyers.

Beyond having an informative website, social media platforms like Instagram, LinkedIn, and Facebook are essential tools for creating a vibrant community around your brand. These platforms allow you to engage directly with your audience through interactive content and meaningful conversations. By sharing a mix of property news, success stories, behind-the-scenes looks, and tips about the real estate process, you invite followers to become part of your narrative, fostering a sense of community and belonging. For instance, using Instagram Stories or Facebook Live to host virtual open houses or Q&A sessions can create an interactive experience that engages potential clients on a more personal level, helping them feel connected to both you and your brand.

Another effective strategy involves utilizing pay-per-click (PPC) advertising and targeted social media ads to expand your reach. PPC campaigns allow you to tailor your advertising efforts to specific demographics, ensuring your message reaches those most likely to benefit from your services. Whether targeting first-time homebuyers in a particular neighborhood or luxury property seekers, these ads can significantly enhance your visibility among your desired client base. With precise targeting options, you can customize your content based on factors such as income levels, geographic location, and interests, making it far more likely that you will attract serious inquiries rather than casual browsers.

Ensuring consistency across all digital channels is vital to reinforcing your brand identity. Develop visual identity guidelines that include color schemes, typography, imagery, and logo usage to maintain uniformity. Crafting a unified message across your website, social media profiles, and advertisements is equally important. This not only reinforces the professionalism of your brand but also makes it instantly recognizable to potential clients. Consistency in your digital presence helps build reliability and trust, which are key components in the decision-making process for clients considering engaging your services.

Moreover, embracing video content as part of your digital strategy can significantly amplify your branding efforts. Video marketing, due to its highly engaging nature, allows for a more dynamic presentation of properties and services. According to The Ultimate Guide to Digital Marketing in Real Estate, video content is expected to dominate web traffic by 2023, underscoring the importance of incorporating this medium into your branding efforts. From virtual tours and neighborhood showcases to customer testimonials and educational content, videos can effectively convey your brand's personality and value proposition in an easily digestible format.

Lastly, incorporating DAER model—Delegate, Automate,

Execute, and Repeat—is crucial. Delegating involves assigning tasks to yourself or scheduling activities, such as setting a specific time, like 8 a.m., for actions in your agenda. Automating refers to establishing an online presence, like a social media page or website, which can attract clients even while you sleep. Executing means implementing your plans swiftly to facilitate a smooth transition to subsequent tasks, and repeating this cycle ensures ongoing effectiveness.

CHAPTER 6

NURTURING CLIENT AND COLLEAGUE RELATIONSHIPS

Cultivating professional connections is crucial for achieving success in the real estate sector. Whether you're new to the field, a budding agent, or transitioning from a different profession, establishing robust relationships with clients and peers creates opportunities for meaningful interactions and business advancement. Central to these connections are communication skills that promote clarity and trust. It all starts with mastering the art of listening—fully understanding what others express and recognizing unspoken concerns. This ability enables real estate agents to connect on a profound level, empowering them to not only fulfill but also foresee client demands.

By being attentive, you demonstrate that others' perspectives are valued, paving the way for enduring partnerships. Remember, winning an argument may inflate your ego, but striving to understand the viewpoints of clients and colleagues enriches dialogue. Be the last to speak, ensuring that your insights linger in their minds.

In this chapter, you'll explore a range of strategies designed to enhance your ability to connect meaningfully with others. Topics such as empathy and managing expectations will be discussed, highlighting how these elements contribute to creating supportive environments where clients feel valued. You'll also delve into the role of non-verbal cues like body language and tone, learning how subtle signals can reinforce messages and build rapport. Beyond client interactions, the chapter addresses ways to strengthen internal team dynamics through transparency and accountability.

As you navigate these themes, you will discover practical approaches for turning one-time clients into repeat customers, ensuring long-term satisfaction, and integrating personal touches into your services. These insights are tailored to equip you with the tools needed to become a trusted and successful agent in the competitive real estate landscape.

ACTIVE LISTENING, EMPATHY, AND MANAGING EXPECTATIONS

In the bustling world of real estate, understanding clients' needs and feelings is more than just a courtesy; it's the foundation for building rapport, trust, and managing expectations effectively. For those new to the field or transitioning from other careers, this skill is essential to set yourself apart in a competitive market.

Active listening stands out as a vital tool in uncovering true client needs. It goes beyond merely hearing words to truly understanding the concerns and desires being expressed. This kind of deep listening builds trust and often reveals underlying issues that might not be apparent at first glance. In practice, active listening empowers real estate professionals to engage with clients more meaningfully.

For instance, when a client expresses worry about moving to a new area, an agent using active listening might pick up on concerns about proximity to schools or workplaces, allowing them to address these fears proactively. By doing so, agents not only meet stated needs but also anticipate and manage future expectations, strengthening the rapport with their clients. According to Call Center Studio, active listening is pivotal because it builds trust and rapport while enhancing problem-solving abilities and reducing misunderstandings (*What Is Active Listening and Its Role in Improving Your Customer Service Quality | Call Center Studio, n.d.*).

Another cornerstone of effective communication in real estate is empathy. An empathetic response does more than just acknowledge a client's emotions; it transforms interactions by creating a supportive environment. This approach fosters loyalty, as clients feel genuinely understood and valued, distinguishing you from competitors who may focus solely on transactions. Imagine a situation where a client is anxious about selling their family home. Responding with empathy—understanding the emotional attachment and providing reassurance—can ease their stress and foster a sense of security. Empathy, therefore, is not just a skill but a strategic advantage in building long-term client relationships.

Non-verbal communication, such as body language and tone, plays a crucial role in reinforcing messages and establishing trust. A warm smile, steady eye contact, or a calm and reassuring tone can significantly impact how messages are received. These non-verbal cues allow agents to tailor their approaches based on client feedback, creating a more personalized and responsive service. For example, maintaining eye contact shows attentiveness, while nodding indicates understanding. When combined with verbal affirmations like "I understand your concern," these subtle cues reinforce sincerity and competence. As emphasized by Call Center Studio, non-verbal communication ensures customers feel heard and valued, enhancing overall satisfaction *(What Is Active Listening and Its Role in Improving Your Customer Service Quality | Call Center Studio, n.d.).*

Clear communication of services and regular updates are fundamental in preventing misunderstandings, setting realistic goals, and ensuring client satisfaction. In real estate, surprises can lead to dissatisfaction and lost trust. By clearly outlining the services you provide and keeping clients informed throughout the process, you prevent miscommunication and align expectations. Regular updates, whether through emails, calls, or meetings, keep clients engaged and confident that their needs are being addressed. This transparency assists in setting realistic goals and fosters an environment where clients feel safe expressing any concerns that may arise. Such practices ensure that all parties remain on the same page, resulting in smoother transactions and heightened client satisfaction.

For aspiring real estate professionals, developing these communication skills requires both awareness and practice. Begin by consciously implementing active listening techniques. Focus on fully engaging with the speaker without interrupting, paraphrasing their concerns to confirm understanding, and responding appropriately.

Practice empathy by recognizing and validating emotions, and utilize non-verbal communication to reinforce sincerity and reliability. Furthermore, maintain clarity in all exchanges, utilizing updates to guide clients through processes confidently. These guidelines give structure to your interactions, helping forge stronger connections and leading to more successful outcomes.

As you continue to cultivate and refine these skills, you will find that they become integral not only to your professional interactions but also to building lasting relationships within the industry. The ability to listen actively, respond empathetically, communicate clearly, and use non-verbal cues effectively equips you to navigate complex situations with poise and professionalism.

Over time, these skills enhance your reputation as a reliable and trustworthy partner, ultimately contributing to your success in the competitive landscape of real estate.

BUILDING TRUST WITH COLLEAGUES AND TURNING CLIENTS INTO REPEAT BUSINESS

In the realm of nurturing professional relationships, transparency in communication stands as a cornerstone for building trust and collaboration. In any environment, especially real estate where transactions require mutual understanding and openness, transparent communication becomes more than just a strategy; it's a necessity.

Transparency involves openly sharing information, decisions, and intentions with colleagues and clients alike. When teams engage transparently, they create an atmosphere conducive to trust and problem-solving. For instance, when everyone on a team is aware of project objectives and potential challenges, it makes addressing issues collectively much easier, thus promoting teamwork efficiency.

To cultivate a culture of transparency, establish regular communication channels within your team. Consider holding weekly meetings for sharing updates or creating digital platforms that make essential information accessible to everyone. By fostering continuous open dialogue, you not only facilitate immediate solutions but also reassure your colleagues that their contributions are appreciated and remembered. Embrace the role of a learn-as-you-go team member; observe what strategies are successful for others. Prioritizing adaptability and active listening over being the most knowledgeable will enhance your skills and benefit the entire team.

Moving from internal dynamics to external client interactions, dependability and accountability are pivotal in establishing credibility. These traits manifest in consistently fulfilling promises, meeting deadlines, and maintaining a high standard of work. In the competitive world of real estate, reputation can make or break professional engagements. Being the agent who always delivers what is promised—or even surpassing expectations—earns respect and trust from clients, making them more likely to seek your services repeatedly.

Accountability is not just about individual actions but extends to organizational practices. A culture of accountability, where every team member takes responsibility for their role in a transaction, creates an environment of reliability. Implementing accountability systems, such as regular performance reviews or feedback sessions, ensures ongoing growth and adherence to commitments. This practice also aligns with fostering a supportive workplace where learning from mistakes is part of the professional journey, ultimately boosting team morale and effectiveness.

Conversely, while structured processes are critical, personalized follow-ups and loyalty programs equally contribute to client retention. Personalization demonstrates care and attention beyond mere transactional relationships. It acknowledges each client's unique needs and preferences, making them feel valued. Sending a simple thank-you note after a deal or checking in months later about their satisfaction with a purchase shows clients you value their satisfaction and opinions.

Loyalty programs might include offering returning clients discounts, exclusive access to new listings, or updates on market trends tailored to their interests. These efforts highlight commitment to their long-term satisfaction and signal that your relationship is not just business-centric but client-oriented. Thus, personalized engagement becomes an integral part of turning one-time clients into loyal customers who return for future transactions and recommend your services to others.

Furthermore, continuous engagement and community-building play vital roles in maintaining strong client connections. Engaging clients should be seen as an ongoing process rather than a task with a finite endpoint. This can be achieved through newsletters, free workshops, or community events that not only keep clients informed but also integrated into a larger network associated with your brand. These activities foster a sense of belonging, reminding clients that they're part of a bigger story woven together by mutual interests and goals.

Creating a client community is particularly effective in real estate, where word-of-mouth referrals and testimonials significantly impact success rates. By positioning yourself not merely as a transactional partner but as a trusted advisor and community builder, you ensure lasting impressions and enduring professional ties. For instance, hosting webinars on property investment tips or inviting clients to exclusive open house not only positions you as a thought leader but keeps your brand top of mind.

CHAPTER 7

ACHIEVING WORK-LIFE BALANCE

Achieving work-life balance is about finding harmony between professional ambitions and personal life commitments. In today's fast-paced world, especially in industries like real estate where demands are high and schedules are unpredictable, maintaining this balance can seem elusive. Often, the thrill of chasing career goals can overshadow personal well-being, leading to stress and burnout. However, achieving a satisfying equilibrium is not just a utopian idea but a practical necessity for sustainable success. The journey toward balance involves not only managing time effectively but also nurturing mental and physical health to ensure that both aspects of life flourish. By understanding the intricate dynamics between work and personal commitments, individuals can develop strategies that promote both productivity and personal joy.

This chapter delves into vital components crucial to this balancing act. It explores the importance of establishing clear boundaries to create a definitive separation between work and personal time, highlighting how these lines prevent burnout and enhance mental wellness. Readers will gain insights into effective boundary-setting techniques, such as defining precise work hours and developing a structured work schedule to minimize distractions.

The chapter also emphasizes the significance of having a designated workspace, which helps maintain focus and reduce stress by marking a psychological boundary between professional tasks and personal life.

Additionally, communication comes under scrutiny as an essential tool to ensure that established boundaries are respected by colleagues and clients alike. Furthermore, the chapter examines integrating health and personal interests into daily routines, offering practical advice on leveraging physical exercise and mindfulness strategies to enhance productivity and mental clarity. Through these insights, readers will learn how to navigate the challenging terrain of the real estate industry while sustaining personal well- being and achieving a meaningful work-life balance.

ESTABLISHING BOUNDARIES AND WELLNESS PRIORITIZATION

Establishing clear boundaries is essential to keep your professional responsibilities from invading your personal life. This requires intentionally marking the beginning and end of your workday. Without these distinctions, work obligations can overlap with personal time, resulting in burnout and reduced productivity. By specifying your work hours, you safeguard your mental well-being and lay the groundwork for effective time management. Always remember: when you work, focus on work; when you're on vacation, fully embrace your time off with your family or loved ones—never mix the two.

Developing a structured work schedule is another vital aspect of establishing boundaries. Defining your work hours encourages a disciplined approach to time management, helping to minimize distractions. When you adhere to a schedule, you're able to allocate focused periods to work tasks and ensure that personal time is preserved. This practice fosters consistent productivity habits and prevents the chaos often associated with multitasking or irregular working hours.

For instance, if you decide your work hours are from 8 am to 6 pm, sticking to this allows you to engage fully in work activities during those hours while completely disengaging outside them. This commitment to structure not only reinforces productivity but also ensures you have time to nurture personal relationships and pursue leisure activities, contributing to overall well-being.

However, if you're just starting as a real estate agent, you have to push yourself to your limits; 8 am to 6 pm will never be enough to gather new clients, learn new skills, etc. Always put in extra work to stay ahead of your competition, which is yourself, but always learn to balance as well.

Having a designated workspace can significantly enhance focus and reduce work-related stress. Designated spaces signal to the brain that it's time to transition into work mode, thereby improving concentration and mental clarity.

In the realm of real estate, where managing multiple tasks

and client interactions is common, having a dedicated space can help separate professional tasks from personal interruptions.

Creating an environment specifically for work tasks means fewer distractions and a clearer mindset, facilitating a more productive workday. Whether it's a specific room or simply a defined corner of your home, this setup tells your brain it's time to be productive once you enter that space, and conversely, to relax and unwind once you leave it. This physical boundary reinforces the mental boundaries we establish when balancing work and personal life.

Communicating your boundaries effectively is key to ensuring they are respected by colleagues, clients, family and friends. When you articulate your availability clearly, it sets expectations and reduces the chance of misunderstandings or conflicts. For real estate professionals constantly interacting with clients and colleagues, this communication builds confidence and strengthens professional relationships.

Letting others know when you are available for work discussions or meetings helps in managing workload efficiently. It's important to convey that outside those hours, barring emergencies, your time is reserved for personal matters. This form of self-advocacy not only enhances respect in professional circles but also empowers you to take control of your work-life balance.

Real-world examples show how effective communication can mitigate work-life conflicts. For instance, setting up automatic email responses indicating your working hours can manage expectations around communication timelines. Similarly, informing clients and colleagues of your preferred modes of after-hours contact (if any) keeps everyone aligned with your boundaries.

INTEGRATING HEALTH AND PERSONAL INTERESTS

In today's fast-paced real estate industry, the pursuit of success often demands a balance between professional ambitions and personal life commitments. One crucial aspect of achieving this balance is enhancing productivity through health and interests. Good physical health is a cornerstone for maintaining high levels of energy and focus throughout your workday. It's well-documented that individuals who prioritize their physical well- being experience reduced risk of burnout and enjoy improved overall well-being (Stults-Kolehmainen & Sinha, 2014). The human body thrives on movement, and engaging in regular physical activity can lead to significant enhancements in both mood and energy levels.

Incorporating simple exercises into your daily routine doesn't require a gym membership or a significant time commitment. Whether it's taking a brisk walk during lunch breaks or doing a short set of stretches between client meetings, these small actions can have a profound impact on your mental clarity and help alleviate feelings of overwhelm.

If you're burned out, take a deep breath and have some sun or go out for a walk with some fresh air, trees, and hummingbirds; this will relax your brain. The repetitive nature of exercise, such as yoga or jogging, can also serve as a meditative practice, offering you a chance to clear your mind and refocus your thoughts.

When physical movement becomes an integral part of your lifestyle, you're not only investing in improved health but also paving the way for greater productivity in your work. To get started, try setting aside just ten minutes each day for a form of exercise you enjoy. Consistency over intensity will yield beneficial results and foster habits that integrate seamlessly into your busy schedule.

In tandem with physical exercise, mindfulness strategies can be powerful tools for navigating the challenges inherent in the real estate market. Mindfulness, which involves being fully present in the current moment, can greatly enhance your resilience when facing obstacles. By practicing mindfulness techniques such as meditation or deep breathing exercises, you develop the ability to stay calm under pressure, make informed decisions, and ultimately increase your effectiveness in both professional and personal realms. These strategies don't need to be time-consuming; even brief, focused sessions can provide significant benefits.

To incorporate mindfulness into your routine, start with a simple five-minute meditation practice daily. You can use guided meditation apps or simply sit quietly, focusing on your breath. Over time, extend these sessions as they become more comfortable.

You'll likely notice an enhanced ability to concentrate on tasks and a marked improvement in your problem-solving skills. This heightened level of awareness enables you to approach each challenge with a clear, focused mind, ensuring you deliver optimal results for your clients and yourself.

Furthermore, proper nutrition plays a pivotal role in sustaining high performance levels. Just as a car requires quality fuel to operate efficiently, your body needs nutritious foods to function at its best. A balanced diet rich in whole foods, lean proteins, and healthy fats provides the necessary nutrients to keep your brain sharp and your body energized.

The link between well-rounded nutrition and cognitive function is well-established; after all, a diet that nourishes your brain can lead to improved memory, better attention span, and sharper decision-making capabilities.

Creating healthy meal plans doesn't have to be intimidating. Begin by incorporating more fruits and vegetables into your meals and snacks. Preparing meals in advance can also support healthier choices and save time during your busy week. Start with one meal per day—perhaps breakfast—and plan to make it nutrient-dense and satisfying. Gradually, you'll find it easier to expand this habit to other meals, supporting better lifestyle choices all around.

Beyond basic nutrition, the integration of self-care activities that encourage relaxation and enjoyment can bolster your mental reserves, allowing you to return to work rejuvenated and ready to meet new challenges. Engage in hobbies or leisure activities that bring you joy, whether that means reading, cooking, or spending time outdoors. These moments of self-care are investments in your long-term productivity, anchoring you firmly in your personal well-being while you pursue professional success.

CHAPTER 8

SUSTAINING SUCCESS

Achieving lasting success in real estate relies on the ability to foster growth while remaining flexible to shifts in the industry. This chapter explores the critical role of ongoing personal and professional advancement, stressing that a complacent approach can result in decline.

By extracting insights from previous encounters, one can establish a solid groundwork for future victories. Reflecting on these moments serves as a potent motivator, especially when recognizing achievements as significant indicators of advancement.

Additionally, consistently evaluating one's performance through constructive feedback acts as a guiding star, illuminating areas for enhancement. Success is not merely about winning; it also involves learning to fail quickly to refine your approach. Furthermore, success isn't a destination; it's a responsibility that must be embraced daily.

Throughout this chapter, you will find insights into crafting a forward-thinking growth plan that remains flexible amid market fluctuations. By embracing adaptability, professionals can not only survive but thrive during times of change. The text provides practical strategies for integrating new technologies, such as AI-driven analytics and virtual reality tours, to enhance client services and streamline operations.

Furthermore, the chapter explores how creativity and collaboration can be valuable tools in addressing industry challenges. It discusses the significance of continuous learning and networking, offering guidance on leveraging educational opportunities and building connections to stay competitive. Through these discussions, readers are equipped with actionable strategies to foster a progressive career in real estate.

CONTEMPLATING PERSONAL AND PROFESSIONAL DEVELOPMENT AND NURTURING SPIRITUAL PRACTICE

Contemplating your journey serves as an invaluable asset that can elevate your future success in real estate. Recognizing and celebrating your career milestones can significantly enhance your drive and self-assurance. These milestones represent more than mere accomplishments; they are benchmarks of the growth you've achieved since embarking on your professional path. By acknowledging these successes, you can leverage them, discerning effective strategies while identifying areas that still need improvement. Additionally, having faith, regardless of your beliefs, can bolster your motivation and confidence, reinforcing the idea that your aspirations are attainable through the belief in a higher power that shapes our existence.

Take a moment to reflect on the moments when you closed your first sale or when you successfully negotiated a difficult deal. These moments are worth remembering as they represent times when your skills and dedication paid off.

Celebrating these career milestones is essential because it reminds you of your capabilities and motivates you to aim higher. When you look back at what you've accomplished, you're able to reinforce your belief in your abilities and fuel your ambition to reach new heights.

While reflecting on past successes is important, understanding yourself through self-assessment tools can play a crucial role in your ongoing development. Feedback from clients and mentors can be particularly insightful. Clients provide an external perspective on your strengths and areas for improvement, while mentors can share their experiences and guide you based on lessons learned from their own careers. Utilizing feedback as a self-assessment tool allows you to identify your core strengths and pinpoint necessary areas for improvement with clarity.

For instance, if multiple clients praise your negotiation skills, consider how you can leverage this strength in upcoming projects. Conversely, if there's feedback indicating difficulties in communication, take steps to improve by seeking further training or mentorship. This adaptive approach ensures that you continually refine your skills, making you more effective in your profession.

Creating a growth plan is another practical step toward sustaining success in real estate. A well- structured growth plan should not only outline your aspirations but must also be adaptable to changes within the industry. The real estate landscape is perpetually evolving due to technological advancements and shifts in market dynamics, and adaptability is key to ensuring that your plans remain relevant and feasible. For instance, if there's a new trend in digital property tours, your growth plan should include learning about this technology and implementing it into your practice. Creating room for flexibility prevents stagnation and keeps you responsive to industry changes.

In your growth strategy, flexibility is essential; it requires a willingness to adjust your direction when needed. If a specific tactic fails to deliver the anticipated outcomes, embrace the opportunity to innovate or eliminate ineffective elements. This mindset keeps you agile and driven, allowing you to seize new possibilities while remaining aligned with your primary objectives. By fostering this adaptability, you guarantee that each action you undertake propels you closer to your ultimate vision of success. Remember, if something isn't working, consider trying a fresh approach or discarding what no longer serves you.

While planning and assessments are integral, documenting your experiences through journaling provides an additional layer of reflection. Journaling your achievements creates a written record of your successes, challenges, and the lessons learned from them. This practice encourages a positive mindset and fosters continuous aspiration by allowing you to see your growth over time. When you document a challenging client interaction and how you resolved it, you create a reference point that can guide you in future similar situations.

Furthermore, journaling can serve as an emotional outlet, helping you process both triumphs and setbacks. It offers a chance to appreciate the small victories that might otherwise go unnoticed amid daily responsibilities. This habit builds resilience and helps maintain focus on your objectives, providing a sense of continuity and purpose in your journey.

STAYING ADAPTABLE IN A CHANGING INDUSTRY

In the dynamic landscape of real estate, staying ahead of industry trends can make the difference between success and stagnation. As technology advances at a rapid pace, early adoption can position real estate professionals well ahead of their competitors. New tools like AI-driven analytics, virtual reality tours, and blockchain transactions are not just futuristic concepts but current realities shaping the market.

Embracing these technologies requires an upfront investment, yet the advantages are clear—streamlined processes, enhanced client experiences, and increased operational efficiency. Such innovations allow professionals to offer more personalized services that cater to the demanding needs of modern clients.

Flexibility in approach is another essential strategy for thriving in real estate. The ability to adapt quickly to changing market conditions transforms obstacles into opportunities. An agent's versatility can turn a declining market into a chance to restructure services, tapping into niche segments previously overlooked. Whether adjusting marketing strategies to appeal to evolving demographics or swiftly responding to economic shifts, flexibility ensures resilience in unpredictable environments. Real estate professionals who cultivate adaptability can navigate challenges such as fluctuating interest rates or shifting consumer preferences, using these to refine their business models for better outcomes.

Moreover, flexibility encourages creativity and opens doors for innovative problem-solving. By fostering a culture that supports collaboration and brainstorming, real estate agents can develop unique solutions to pressing issues. This innovative mindset not only enhances competitiveness but also leads to new market propositions. Collaborative efforts might involve partnerships with other professionals in the field, sharing insights and resources to benefit all parties involved. These alliances can create pathways to untapped markets, offering products or services tailored to specific client needs.

Creativity and collaboration also play a vital role in addressing complex problems within the industry. For instance, when faced with high property prices deterring first-time buyers, innovative financing options or shared ownership schemes can provide viable alternatives. By pooling ideas from diverse team members or external partners, agencies can devise fresh tactics to tackle longstanding barriers, making real estate more accessible and attractive to a broader audience.

Continuous learning remains a cornerstone for sustaining success within this fast-paced industry. Engaging in advanced training courses and attending industry workshops are critical to keeping skills sharp and up-to-date. This commitment to lifelong education gives professionals a competitive advantage, enabling them to serve clients with confidence and expertise.

Moreover, staying informed about the latest regulations, market trends, and technological advancements positions agents as knowledgeable advisors who clients can trust.

The benefits of continuous learning extend beyond skill

enhancement. Networking opportunities often accompany educational events, allowing professionals to build valuable connections within the industry. These networks can lead to collaborative ventures, mentorships, and even new client referrals, further fortifying one's standing in the market. Additionally, engaging with peers during conferences or seminars exposes agents to different perspectives and inspires innovative ideas that can be applied to their practice.

To fully embrace industry trends, maintain flexibility, foster innovation, and commit to continuous learning, real estate professionals need actionable guidelines. First, they should consider setting clear objectives for technology adoption, focusing on tools that align with their long-term business strategy. It's effective to start small, implementing one or two changes initially and measuring their impact before expanding to larger-scale integration. Regularly assessing the effectiveness of new technologies helps identify what truly adds value to operations and enhances client satisfaction.

Cultivating an adaptable mindset requires fostering transparent communication within teams and encouraging a readiness to explore innovative methods. Establishing an atmosphere where employees feel empowered to propose and experiment with fresh ideas nurtures a culture of innovation that seeks growth beyond conventional limits. Conducting regular meetings to examine market shifts and collaboratively develop responsive strategies ensures everyone remains connected and well-informed. Once you become an expert in your field, always share your knowledge with newcomers, as every master was once a novice.

REFERENCES

2024 Career Goals for Real Estate Agents - 12+ Goal Examples (Full Guide). (n.d.). www.tealhq.com.

https://www.tealhq.com/professional-goals/real-estate-agent

Self-Assessment Tools for Professional Development: Best Practices. (n.d.). Hrbrain.ai.

https://hrbrain.ai/blog/self-assessment-tools-for-professional-development-best-practices/

Team, E. (2024, May 6). *The importance of self- assessments for employees and managers.* Ethena.

https://www.goethena.com/post/the-importance-of-self-assessments-for-employees-and-managers/

admin. (2022, February 2). *9 Real Estate Goals for Success for Agents and Investors.* Wise Pelican.

https://wisepelican.com/top-7-real-estate-goals/?srsltid=AfmBOop7MoavgdJ8u4PQZlXzfnfJh8sLFYNiz7L5RQXno8vsgOnItqMt

Arlinghaus, K. R., & Johnston, C. A. (2018, December 29). *The Importance of Creating Habits and Routine. American Journal of Lifestyle Medicine.*

https://doi.org/10.1177/1559827618818044

Cherry, K. (2020). *The Importance of Maintaining Structure and Routine During Stressful Times.* Verywell Mind.

https://www.verywellmind.com/the-importance-of-keeping-a-routine-during- stressful-times-4802638

Drummond, J. (2023, September 15). *7 Ways to Build Resilience at Work - Jenn Drummond.* Jenn Drummond.

https://jenndrummond.com/blog/7-ways-to-build-resilience-at-work/

Team, P. (2024, September 17). *How Leaders Overcome Challenges and Build Workplace Resilience.* Pareto.co.uk; Pareto UK.

https://www.pareto.co.uk/blog-details/how-leaders-overcome-challenges-and-build-workplace- resilience/

Building a professional network online: How to connect with your peers and working professionals in a virtual environment | Penn LPS Online. (2024, May 15). Lpsonline.sas.upenn.edu.

https://lpsonline.sas.upenn.edu/features/building-professional-network-online

Kaado, B. (2022, August 5). *How to Grow Your Professional Network - businessnewsdaily.com.* Business News Daily.

https://www.businessnewsdaily.com/4363-tips-build-professional-network.html

Seed, A. (2024, June 26). *Business Networking: Strategies for Making Effective Connections – Lawrence County Chamber of Commerce.* Lawrence County Chamber of Commerce.

https://lawrencecountychamberofcommerce.info/business-networking-strategies-for-making-effective- connections/

Vera, D. D. (2024, February 10). *12 Effective Networking Strategies for Small Business Owners and Entrepreneurs. CFO Consultants, LLC |* Trusted Financial Consultants.

https://cfoconsultants.net/12-effective-networking-strategies-for-small-business-owners-and- entrepreneurs/

Chauhan, A., Begum, J., Lavanya, K. M., Gupta, A., & Kulkarni, S. (2024, November 1). *Experiential Learning of Active Learning Strategies in Mentor Learner Web-based Discussions: A Perceptions Study.* International Journal of Applied and Basic Medical Research; Medknow Publications. https://doi.org/10.4103/ijabmr.ijabmr_277_24

Characteristics of Mentoring Relationships | Youth.gov. (n.d.). Youth.gov.

https://youth.gov/youth-topics/mentoring/characteristics-mentoring-relationships

Key Features of an Effective Mentoring Relationship. (n.d.). The Center for Faculty Excellence at the GW School of Medicine and Health Sciences.

https://cfe.smhs.gwu.edu/key-features-effective-mentoring-relationship

Ryan, E. (2020, February 3). *Active Listening: The Most Important Skill for Effective Mentors.* Mentorloop Mentoring Software.

https:// mentorloop.com/blog/active-listening/

The Ultimate Guide to Digital Marketing in Real Estate . (n.d.). Proven Partners.

https://www.proven.partners/blog/digital-marketing-real-estate

The new real estate investment edge: Tech-enabled brand, CX, and loyalty | McKinsey. (n.d.). www.mckinsey.com.

https://www.mckinsey.com/industries/real-estate/our-insights/the-new-real-estate-investment-edge-tech-enabled-brand-cx-and-loyalty

https://www.facebook.com/iamTristanAhumada.

(2024, July 15). *Networking for Real Estate Agents: Connections and Differentiation Strategies | A Brilliant Tribe*. A Brilliant Tribe. https://abrillianttribe.com/networking-for-real-estate-agents-connections-and-differentiation-strategies/

\r\n \n *Crafting Your Unique Value Proposition: A Realtor's Guide to Standing Out*\n \r\n. (2022). Kwadvisorseastbay.com.

https://www.kwadvisorseastbay.com/crafting-your-unique-value-proposition-a-realtor-s-guide-to- standing-out

Author, G. (2023, March 21). *Leadership Tips: Trust and Transparency.* Cleanfax.

https://cleanfax.com/trust-and-transparency/

Grossman, D. (2024, April 8). *Trust in the Workplace: 6 Steps to Building Trust with Employees* Yourthoughtpartner.com. https://www.yourthoughtpartner.com/blog/bid/59619/leaders-follow-these-6-steps-to-build-trust-with-employees-improve-how-you-re-perceived

Pollack, J. (2024, May 23). *Active Listening in Customer Service: Importance, Skills & Examples.* Peaceful Leaders Academy.

https://peacefulleadersacademy.com/blog/active-listening-customer-service/

What is Active Listening and Its Role in Improving Your Customer Service Quality | Call Center Studio. (n.d.).

https://callcenterstudio.com/blog/what-is-active-listening-and-its-role-in-improving-your-customer-service-quality/

Navigating Work-Life Balance: Tips for Preventing Burnout in the Modern Workplace. (n.d.).

www.corporatewellnessmagazine.com. https://www.corporatewellnessmagazine.com/article/navigating-work-life-balance-tips-for- preventing-burnout-in-the-modern-workplace

Stults-Kolehmainen, M. A., & Sinha, R. (2014). *The Effects of Stress on Physical Activity and Exercise.* Sports Medicine. https://doi.org/10.1007/s40279-013-0090-5

Zimmerman, C. (2024, February 15). *Beat Burnout: 7 Key Strategies for a Balanced Life* | Counseling Associates for Well-Being.

https://ca4wellbeing.com/7-ways-to-prevent-burnout/adminadmin.

(2024, September 23). *Boosting Productivity: The Power of Mindfulness and Self-Care - TLEX Mind Matters.* TLEX Mind Matters.

https://tlexmindmatters.com/blog/boosting- productivity/

Adapting to Market Trends: Staying Relevant in a Dynamic Real Estate Landscape. (2024). Ronkoenigsberg.com.

https://www.ronkoenigsberg.com/blog/adapting-to-market-trends-staying-relevant-in-a-dynamic-real-estate-landscape

Mehta, S. (2024, April 23). *Real Estate Technology Trends to Watch Out for in 2024.* REsimpli.

https://resimpli.com/blog/real-estate-technology/

Plahonina, M. (2023, November 13). *The Art Of Personal Reflection: Nurturing Professional Growth* | REVERB.

https://reverbico.com/blog/the-art-of-personal-reflection-nurturing-professional-growth/

Ryan, E. (2019, July 29). *Reflection on Work Improves Career Performance* – Mentorloop. Mentorloop Mentoring Software.

https:// mentorloop.com/blog

ABOUT THE AUTHOR

Kenneth Leonardo began his career working on a cruise ship for six years before making a significant career shift in 2021 to join the real estate industry. Despite lacking prior knowledge and expertise, he quickly became one of the top property consultants at Megaworld Corporation, achieving an impressive gross sales figure of 292 million in his first year. His success can be attributed to his adept use of digital selling techniques, which allowed him to attract clients from around the globe.

You may reach him through . . .

Facebook:
https://www.facebook.com/maplegrovemegaworldcavite/

LinkedIn:
https://www.linkedin.com/in/kennethleonardo/

www.ingramcontent.com/pod-product-compliance
Lightning Source LLC
Chambersburg PA
CBHW071056240526
45469CB00006BD/2325